THE REAL
Typhoid Mary

45th Parallel Press

Published in the United States of America by Cherry Lake Publishing
Ann Arbor, Michigan
www.cherrylakepublishing.com

Reading Adviser: Marla Conn MS, Ed., Literacy specialist, Read-Ability, Inc.
Book Designer: Felicia Macheske

Photo Credits: © Everett Collection/Shutterstock.com, cover, 1, 19, 20, 23; © Bettmann/Getty Images, 5;
© PointImages/Shutterstock.com, 7; © Kateryna Kon/Shutterstock.com, 9; © Harkin Burke/Shutterstock.com, 11;
© Emiliano Rodriguez/Shutterstock.com, 12; © Yuriy Vahlenko/Shutterstock.com, 15; © Mila Atkovska/
Shutterstock.com, 17; © craetive/iStock.com, 24; © Robert Crum/Shutterstock.com, 27; © Sherry V Smith/
Shutterstock.com, 29; © Nataliia Nata/Shutterstock.com, 30

Graphic Elements Throughout: © iulias/Shutterstock.com; © Thinglass/Shutterstock.com; © kzww/Shutterstock.
com; © A_Lesik/Shutterstock.com; © MegaShabanov/Shutterstock.com; © Groundback Atelier/Shutterstock.com;
© saki80/Shutterstock.com

45th Parallel Press is an imprint of Cherry Lake Publishing.

Library of Congress Cataloging-in-Publication Data

Names: Loh-Hagan, Virginia, author. | Loh-Hagan, Virginia. History uncut.
Title: The real Typhoid Mary / by Virginia Loh-Hagan.
Other titles: Typhoid Mary
Description: Ann Arbor, MI : Cherry Lake Publishing, [2018] | Series: History
  uncut | Audience: Grades 7 to 8. | Includes bibliographical references and
  index.
Identifiers: LCCN 2018004557| ISBN 9781534129511 (hardcover) | ISBN
  9781534132719 (pbk.) | ISBN 9781534131217 (pdf) | ISBN 9781534134416
  (hosted ebook)
Subjects: LCSH: Typhoid Mary, 1869-1938—Juvenile literature. | Cooks—New
  York (State)—New York—Biography—Juvenile literature. | Typhoid
  fever—New York (State)—New York—History—Juvenile literature. |
  Quarantine—New York (State)—New York—History—Juvenile literature.
Classification: LCC RA644.T8 L64 2018 | DDC 614.5/112/092 [B] —dc23
LC record available at https://lccn.loc.gov/2018004557

Cherry Lake Publishing would like to acknowledge the work of The Partnership for 21st Century Skills.
Please visit www.p21.org for more information.

Printed in the United States of America
Corporate Graphics

Table of Contents

Chapter 1
Typhoid Mary
The Story You Know 4

Chapter 2
Coming to America 6

Chapter 3
Tracked Down! 10

Chapter 4
Trapped! 14

Chapter 5
Caught Again! 18

Chapter 6
Unfair World 22

Chapter 7
Alone in Life and Death 26

Timeline 30

Consider This! 31
Learn More 31
Glossary 32
Index 32
About the Author 32

Typhoid Mary
The Story You Know

Mary Mallon was known as "Typhoid Mary." She was a cook. She infected more than 50 people. She gave them typhoid fever. At least 3 people died.

Typhoid fever is a bad sickness. It can be deadly. It causes high fevers. It upsets stomachs. It causes headaches. It causes red spots on the skin. It's spread by eating food or drinking water handled by someone who has it.

Mallon was the first known healthy carrier. Carriers have the sickness. They pass it to others. But Mallon wasn't sick. She didn't have any symptoms. Symptoms are signs of sickness.

Mallon was seen as bad. But there's more to her story…

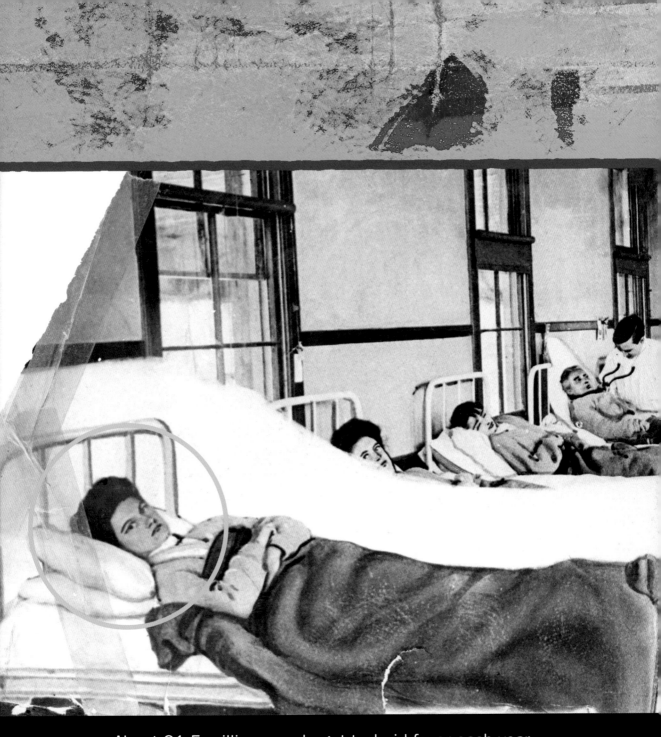

About 21.5 million people get typhoid fever each year.
They're mostly from third-world countries.

CHAPTER 2

Coming to America

Mallon was born on September 23, 1869. She was born in Cookstown, Ireland. She was poor. Some people think she must have had typhoid fever. She had it as a young child. She was too young to remember. She got better. She lived.

Life was tough in Ireland. She **immigrated** to the United States. Immigrate means to move. Mallon wanted a better life. She traveled by herself. She was 15 years old. She lived in New York City. She lived with her aunt and uncle.

Life was tough in New York. Many immigrants came during this time. They were poor. Many people lived in a small area. This spread sickness.

Mallon was a cook from Cookstown.

SETTING THE WORLD STAGE

1869

› Ulysses S. Grant was a Civil War hero. He was a general. He fought for the North. He was elected the 18th president of the United States. In 1869, he was sworn in. Eight full divisions of the army marched in his parade. This was the largest to do so.

› Armand David was a priest. He was also a scientist. He studied animals. He was the first westerner to see a giant panda. This happened in 1869. David was in China. Hunters brought him the panda's body. He saved the skin. He sent it to the National Museum of Natural History in Paris. The panda bear was called "Father David's Bear."

› The National Woman Suffrage Association was formed in 1869. It was formed by Susan B. Anthony and Elizabeth Cady Stanton. It was formed in New York City. It fought for women's rights. It supported women getting the right to vote.

Mallon wasn't educated. She didn't have any skills. She didn't have many choices. She worked as a maid. She was a good cook. Cooks got more money than maids.

She worked for a family in Westchester County, New York. A houseguest got sick. Mallon left. This happened in 1900. Then, Mallon worked for a family in Manhattan. A fellow worker got sick. Mallon worked at 8 different houses. Seven of those houses had **outbreaks**. Outbreaks are when many people get sick at the same time. Mallon quit whenever someone got sick.

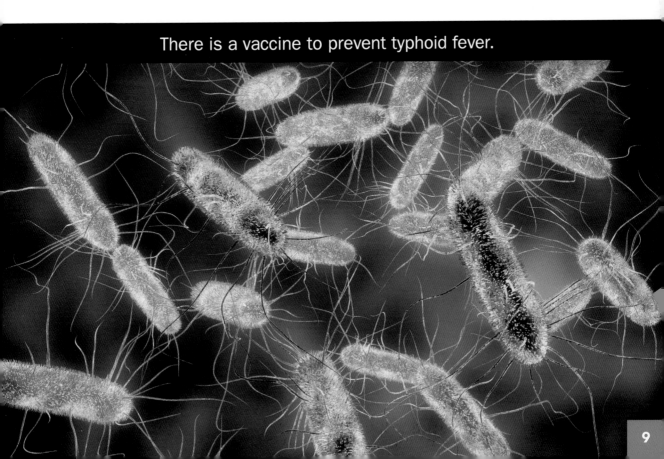

There is a vaccine to prevent typhoid fever.

CHAPTER 3

Tracked Down!

In 1906, Mallon worked in Oyster Bay, Long Island. Six of the 11 family members got sick. Mallon ran away.

George A. Soper was in charge of public health. He was hired to this case. He needed to find out why people were getting sick. He checked for spoiled food. He checked for poisoned water. He couldn't find anything wrong. So, he suspected a human carrier. He learned the cook ran away. This set him on Mallon's trail.

He learned more about Mallon. He found out where she had worked. He made connections. He thought Mallon was a carrier. But he needed proof. He needed to find Mallon.

Typhoid fever was unusual in Oyster Bay.
It was connected with poor areas, not rich ones.

He wanted to help her. He thought she didn't know. He wanted her to stop spreading the sickness. He found her at her new job. He planned a **raid**. Raids are attacks. He confronted Mallon. Mallon denied everything. She fought against him. Soper said, "We were unable to make any **headway**." Headway means progress.

Soper went to the health department. He wanted to force Mallon to be tested. In 1907, a team went to arrest Mallon. Mallon slammed the door on them. She ran. She hid. She was found. She fought.

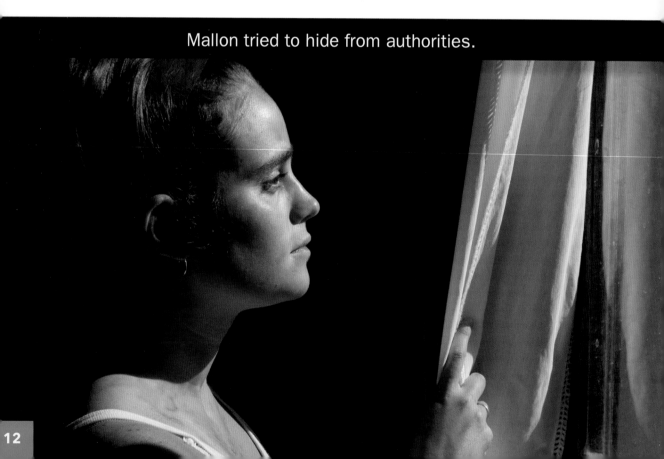

Mallon tried to hide from authorities.

All in the Family

Mallon didn't have a family of her own. She worked for many families. When she was caught, she worked for the Warren family. Charles Henry Warren was a New York banker. He was president of the Lincoln Bank. He rented a summer house in 1906. He rented a place in Oyster Bay, Long Island. The house belonged to George Thompson. Warren hired Mallon as their cook for the summer. One of Warren's daughters got sick. Then, Mrs. Warren and 2 maids got sick. Next, the gardener and another daughter got sick. The first person got sick on August 27, 1906. The last person to get sick was on September 3, 1906. They all had typhoid fever. Two of them were sent to the hospital. Town doctors took care of the others.

"My own doctors say I have no typhoid germs. I am an innocent human being. I have committed no crime and I am treated like an outcast, a criminal. It is unjust, outrageous, uncivilized." – Mary Mallon

CHAPTER 4

Trapped!

Mallon was taken to a hospital. Her blood was tested. Her poop was tested. Her pee was tested. There was typhoid fever in her poop. Soper had his proof. He said, "When she prepared a meal, the germs were washed and rubbed from her fingers into the food. No housekeeper ever gave me to understand that Mary was a particularly clean cook." Mallon admitted to having poor **hygiene**. Hygiene is the act of staying clean. Mallon said she didn't know why she had to wash her hands.

The health department had to protect the city. They didn't want anyone else getting sick. They put Mallon away for 3 years.

People didn't wash as much as we do today.

THAT Happened?!?

Sicknesses have a smell. People with typhoid smell like freshly baked brown bread. The smell comes out of their body parts. It comes out of their skin. It comes out of their breath. It comes out of their pee. It comes out of their blood. Scientists study body smells. They do tests. They collect body odors. They smell armpits. They smell shirts. They smell breath. They smell pee. They smell poop. They compare healthy to sick people. They study how strong the smells are. They study how sweet the smells are. They study how gross the smells are. They found that smells from sick people are the worst.

"I have been, in fact, a peep show for everybody."
— Mary Mallon

Mallon was taken to North Brother Island. This island housed people with **contagious** sicknesses. Contagious means easily spread. Mallon felt like she was in jail. She lived in a small house. She was away from people.

Mallon was mad. She felt healthy. She didn't break any laws. She had been taken by force. She had been taken against her will. She was being held without a trial.

In 1909, Mallon **sued**. Sued means to take legal action. Mallon fought for her freedom. She lost. Some people think William Randolph Hearst paid for her lawyer. Hearst was a rich man. He owned newspapers. He knew Mallon's story would sell papers.

Mallon only had a dog to keep her company on North Brother Island.

CHAPTER 5

Caught Again!

In 1910, Mallon was allowed to leave North Brother Island. But there were rules. She couldn't work as a cook again. She had to practice good hygiene. She had to keep in contact with the health department.

She got a job cleaning clothes. This didn't pay much. Mallon needed more money. She had no other skills. She had to cook again. She changed her name. She became Mary Brown. She worked in several houses. There were outbreaks.

In 1915, Mallon worked at Sloane Hospital for Women. Twenty-five workers got sick. Two people died. Soper was on the case again. He found Mallon. He said, "She was a dangerous character and must be treated accordingly."

Poor Irish immigrant women didn't have many choices at this time.

Mallon was taken to North Brother Island again. She had little hope of freedom. She was now seen as a criminal. She broke her **parole**. Parole is the rules for release. Mallon put people's lives at risk.

So, how did Mary spread the sickness? She'd use the bathroom. She wouldn't wash her hands. She'd handle food. Cooking food in high heat would kill germs. But Mallon's most popular dish wasn't cooked. She made ice cream. She cut up peaches. She froze the peaches in the ice cream. She passed her germs into the dessert. People ate it. They got sick.

Mallon became famous. Newspapers wanted to interview her.

Bad Blood

Mallon's enemy was George A. Soper. Soper is famous for tracking her down. He wasn't being mean. He was just doing his job. Soper was born in 1870. He died on June 17, 1948. He was a sanitation engineer. Sanitation means the act of keeping things clean. Soper's job was to protect the public health. He managed the city's dirty water. He managed the city's sewer system. He studied at Rensselaer Polytechnic Institute. He also studied at Columbia University. He got a doctorate. Doctorates are the highest degrees people can earn from school. He helped lead the American Cancer Society. He did this from 1923 to 1928. He wanted to fight against diseases. He wanted to keep people safe and healthy. He used the latest tools. He used the latest processes.

"I never had typhoid in my life and have always been healthy. Why should I be banished like a leper and compelled to live in solitary confinement with only a dog for a companion?" – Mary Mallon

CHAPTER 6

Unfair World

Mallon said, "It seems incredible that in a Christian community a **defenseless** woman can be treated in this manner." Defenseless means weak.

Mallon didn't understand typhoid fever. She didn't get how she could be a carrier. She seemed healthy. It didn't make sense to her. And no one tried to teach her. Some people think Mallon was treated unfairly. She was a woman. She was Irish. She was poor. She was a maid. She had a temper. She didn't behave like a nice lady. She fought back.

Mallon was in the lower class.

There were other healthy typhoid carriers. First, there was "Typhoid John." John was a mountain guide. He worked in the Adirondack Mountains. John infected 36 tourists. At least 2 people died. Second, there was Tony Labella. Labella was an Italian immigrant. He lived in New York City. He infected many more people than Mallon. He caused 2 outbreaks. Third, there was Alphonse Cotils. Cotils was born in Belgium. He moved to New York. He owned a bakery. He handled food. He infected many people.

None of these men were taken away. Only Mallon was locked up for years. Only Mallon was forced from her life.

◀ There was no law that made it legal to lock up healthy people.

CHAPTER 7

Alone in Life and Death

Mallon didn't cooperate. She took on fake names. She moved around a lot. She had many jobs. She didn't follow rules. There could be more infected than known. There was only one way to protect people. Mallon had to be locked up.

She spent the rest of her life on North Brother Island. She lived there for 23 more years. After a few years, she earned some freedoms. She worked in a lab. She washed bottles. She helped in the hospital. She took short trips to the city. She visited friends for a short time. She cooked and ate alone. She spent more than half her life this way.

Her house had 1 room.

Explained by
SCIENCE

Many sicknesses are spread from dirty hands. Sick people cough. They sneeze. They wipe snot. They use the bathroom. Poop has a lot of germs. A tiny bit of human poop has a trillion germs. These germs can make people sick. Sick germs get on their hands. Then, people touch things. They shake hands. They touch their eyes, noses, and mouths. Germs get into their bodies this way. This spreads germs. People get sick. Washing hands is important. It removes germs from hands. It can stop people from being sick. It can stop the spreading of germs. People must wash with soap. They must wash with clean, running water. They must wash for at least 10 seconds. They must clean under fingernails. They must clean their thumbs. They must clean the folds in palms. They must clean the backs of hands.

In 1932, Mallon had **strokes**. Strokes are brain attacks. This left her **paralyzed**. Paralyzed means not being able to move. She had to move out of her small house. She was moved into a hospital bed. She was moved into the children's area. She stayed there for 6 years. She got **pneumonia**. This is a lung infection. Mallon died on November 11, 1938.

Mallon was cremated. This means her body was burned. Her ashes were buried in the Bronx. Her headstone reads "Jesus Mercy." She had a lonely death. Only 9 people went to her funeral. Because of Mallon, doctors learned more about healthy carriers.

Mallon did not die of typhoid fever.

Timeline

1869   Mallon was born in Northern Ireland. Her town is known for its weaving.

1883   Mallon immigrated to New York. She lived in Queens.

1900   Mallon worked in Mamaroneck, New York. Within 2 weeks, people got sick.

1901   Mallon worked in Manhattan. Family members got sick. The laundress died. A laundress is a person who cleans clothes.

1906   Mallon worked for the Warren family. She worked in a summer home in Oyster Bay.

1907   Mallon was caught for the first time. She was working for the Bowen family.

1907   Mallon was arrested by the health department. The team was led by Dr. S. Josephine Baker. She had to sit on Mallon on the way to the hospital. Baker's father had died of typhoid fever.

1907   Mallon was photographed in the hospital. This is a famous picture. It's one of the few pictures of her.

1907   Mallon was sent to North Brother Island.

1908   Mallon was in the newspapers. She was called Typhoid Mary.

1909   Mallon made her first legal attempt to set herself free.

1909   Mallon wrote a letter to her lawyer. Her lawyer was George Francis O'Neill.

1909   Mallon's appeal was denied. She was sent back to North Brother Island.

1910   Mallon was released. She promised not to cook again.

1915   Mallon was discovered at Sloane Hospital for Women and sent back to North Brother Island. She had been hired as a cook. The workers called her Typhoid Mary. They didn't know she was the real deal.

1922   Mallon helped in the hospital at North Brother Island. She was called a "nurse" or "hospital helper."

1938   Mallon died. She was 69 years old. Scientists found live typhoid germs in her gallbladder.

Consider This!

Take a Position! Some people think Mary Mallon was a bad citizen. They think she put people at risk. Some people think she was treated badly. They think her rights were violated. What do you think? Argue your point with reasons and evidence.

Say What? Learn more about typhoid. Explain what it is. Explain the causes. Explain the effects.

Think About It! People get sick. Some sicknesses can be deadly. Today, people get vaccines. Vaccines are special medicines. They stop people from being sick. What do you do to avoid being sick?

Learn More

Bartoletti, Susan Campbell. *Terrible Typhoid Mary: A True Story of the Deadliest Cook in America*. Boston: Houghton Mifflin Harcourt, 2015.

Jarrow, Gail. *Fatal Fever: Tracking Down Typhoid Mary*. Honesdale, PA: Calkins Creek, 2015.

Morley, Jacqueline, and David Antram (illust.). *You Wouldn't Want to Meet Typhoid Mary!: A Deadly Cook You'd Rather Not Know*. New York: Franklin Watts, 2013.

Glossary

carrier (KAR-ee-ur) a person who has a sickness and spreads it

contagious (kuhn-TAY-juhs) easily spread

defenseless (dih-FENS-les) weak

headway (HED-way) progress

hygiene (HYE-jeen) the act of keeping clean by washing, bathing, etc.

immigrated (IM-ih-grate-id) moved to another country

outbreaks (OUT-brakes) when many people get sick at the same time

paralyzed (PAR-uh-lyzd) not able to move

parole (puh-ROLE) rules from release from jail

pneumonia (noo-MOHN-yuh) a lung infection

raid (RAYD) an attack or invasion

strokes (STROHKS) brain attacks

sued (SOOD) took legal action

symptoms (SIMP-tuhmz) signs of sickness

typhoid (TYE-foid) a sickness or disease that causes high fevers, nausea, headaches, and red spots, and that is spread by eating food or drinking water handled by someone who has it

Index

Anthony, Susan B., 8
food, 4, 10, 14, 20, 25
Grant, Ulysses S., 8
hygiene, 14, 18
Ireland (Irish), 6, 19, 22, 30
Labella, Tony, 25

Mallon, Mary, 4, 6, 7, 9, 10, 12–14, 16–18, 20–23, 25–27, 29, 30, 31
New York City, 6, 8, 25, 29, 30
North Brother Island, 17, 18, 20, 26, 30

Soper, George A., 10, 12, 14, 18, 21
Stanton, Elizabeth Cady, 8
symptoms, 4
typhoid, 4–6, 9, 11, 13, 14, 16, 21, 22, 25, 29, 30, 31

About the Author

Dr. Virginia Loh-Hagan is an author, university professor, former classroom teacher, and curriculum designer. She would love to have a personal chef, but not Typhoid Mary. She lives in San Diego with her very tall husband and very naughty dogs. To learn more about her, visit www.virginialoh.com.